STUDY G[UIDE]

Based on the acclaimed feature f[ilm]

A Heart Transformed Can Change the World

KENNETH CAIN KINGHORN

Abingdon Press
Nashville

Wesley: A Heart Transformed Can Change the World
Study Guide

This book is printed on acid-free paper.

**Library of Congress Cataloging-in-Publication Data
has been ordered**

ISBN 978-1-4267-1885-4

11 12 13 14 15 16 17 18 19 20—10 9 8 7 6 5 4 3 2 1

MANUFACTURED IN THE UNITED STATES OF AMERICA

Contents

Preface

Since John Wesley's birth more than three hundred years ago—Wesley lived from 1703 to 1791—many changes have happened in the world. The eighteenth century was without such benefits as light bulbs, cell phones, computers, automobiles, sewing machines, pasteurization, or antiseptics. Imagine living in a world without aspirin, bandages, email—you get the picture. Clothing tastes are different, as are fashions in music, art, and philosophy. Science and technology have advanced exponentially, as have farming and manufacturing. Since Wesley's time, nature's forces have altered coastlines. New nations have been born; older nations have been torn asunder.

Nonetheless, the fundamental aspects of human life remain constant. We love; we work; we die. Our essential being remains unchanged, and our responses to problems and challenges tend to take the same course as those in previous generations. Undeniably, our society faces obstructions and opportunities strikingly similar to those in John Wesley's time. But above all else, God is unchanging. As the writer of the Letter to the Hebrews states:

> You, Lord, laid the earth's foundations in the beginning,
>   and the heavens are made by your hands.
> They will pass away,
>   but you remain.
> They will all wear out like old clothes.
>   You will fold them up like a coat.

They will be changed like a person changes clothes,
   but you stay the same,
   and the years of your life won't come to an end.
(Hebrews 1:10-12 CEB)

Scripture tells us that Jesus Christ is the same yesterday and today and forever. We can say with certainty that God and humankind have not really changed through the unfolding millennia. Rightly applied, an oft-quoted proverb is true: "The more things change, the more they stay the same."

John Wesley made no pretensions of being a theological innovator. He insisted that he preached only the ageless truths of the Bible. He set forth the fundamental and indispensable truths of biblical revelation, which he declared were "as fixed as the sun." If Wesley did not invent theological novelties, he appropriated biblical truth and the collective wisdom of the Church. He believed that the best way to know God was to practice what he already knew about God, and that we can best understand God by experiencing him.

Wesley refused to split hairs about minor doctrinal debates. Concerning nonessential theological matters, he was content "to think and let think." A cleric wrote him to ask in what ways he differed from the Church, by which he meant the Church of England. He replied, "In none from that part of the clergy who adhere to the doctrines of the church; but from that part of the clergy who dissent from the church (though they own it not)." Wesley said that he preached "the plain old religion of the church, which is now almost everywhere spoken against."

In Wesley's day, political leaders were often corrupt. Popular amusements were crude and vulgar, and commercial entertainment lacked principled restraint. John Wesley declared that the theater in his time was "the sink of all profaneness and debauchery." Public drunkenness was widespread, much of the literature was shallow, and decadent sexual behavior undercut family stability. The rich and strong exploited the poor and weak. In his homeland, England, the cities of Bristol and Liverpool were busy ports for slave-trading, and British prisons were sinkholes of misery. England's established Church was ineffective in improving moral and social conditions.

Rationalism dominated the universities. Many intellectuals prized "reason and moderation" more than the plain teaching of Scripture. They frowned on religious zeal and supernatural considerations. It was said that the two favorite sermon texts for numerous clergymen were "Let your moderation be known to all men" and "Be not righteous overmuch." Many eighteenth-century English preachers were indubitably ignorant of spiritual truth, and they expressed skepticism about the truth claims of Scripture. They sought to construct only a "religion of reason."

Dereliction of clerical duty was rampant in Wesley's day. At one point, 332 parsons shared 1,496 parishes, which they rarely, if ever, visited. The Bishop of Llandaff lived almost all his life at Windermere, while holding a university chair at Cambridge and fourteen other livings in Shropshire and Leicestershire. Another clergyman held two yearly livings worth £1,200 and hired two curates to care for the churches for a total of £84.

Many members of the upper classes were willing for the churches to survive, although they wanted no part of zealous faith or religious "enthusiasm." One of England's freethinkers was asked why he sent his servants to church, even though he himself did not attend. He replied, "That they may neither rob nor murder me." In sum, the rationalists and deists did not look to revealed religion as unfolded in the biblical revelation. Rather, they looked to human reason, boasted of their own philosophical inventions, and denied many of the truths of classical Christianity. Especially, they repudiated the ideas of miracles, faith, and God's involvement in human affairs.

Many clergymen focused on ecclesiastical politics and the maintenance of institutional religion—to the neglect of the transforming power of Christian experience and the reality of a personal relationship with Jesus Christ. A satirist said of one of Britain's best-known clergymen: "He is a retailer of second-hand commonplaces, who gives us the impression that the real man has vanished, and [has] left nothing but a wig and gown."

Many sermons of the day can be described as metaphysical musing and moralizing. These sermonic addresses tended to emphasize what *we* should do for God, rather than what *God* wants to do for us. In short, much religion of the day was not God-centered, but human-centered. A scholar of the eighteenth century later asked rhetorically:

"Of what inspiration . . . was this religious pedantry to the miner in the bowels of the earth, to the mechanic amidst the grime and sweat of the workshop, or to the foundryman daily facing an inferno of flame?" A French proponent of rationalism who visited England said, "In France I was thought to have too little religion, but in England I was thought to have too much religion." The church's ineffective leadership had led to a serious decline in national morals and manners.

When John Wesley first visited Newcastle-on-Tyne, he was shocked by its moral and cultural depravity: "I was surprised; so much drunkenness, cursing, and swearing (even from the mouths of little children) do I never remember to have seen and heard before, in so small a compass of time." He said, "Surely this place is ripe for Him, who came not to call the righteous, but sinners to repentance." Wesley was gripped with the overwhelming reality that many people were perishing in their sins. And he believed God had called him to proclaim a clear call to repentance and faith in Christ, the world's only Savior.

Wesley countered rationalism and clerical incompetence with a ringing articulation of the fundamental realities of the gospel. He maintained that divine revelation does not contradict reason but transcends it. Wesley stated his mission this way:

> I design plain truth for plain people: Therefore, of set purpose, I abstain from all . . . philosophical speculations; from all perplexed and intricate reasonings; and, as far as possible, from

even the show of learning. . . . I labour to avoid all words
which are not easy to be understood, all which are not used in
common life; and, in particular, those kinds of technical terms
that so frequently occur in Bodies of Divinity.

John Wesley was joined by his brother Charles, George
Whitefield, and a good number of lay people to spread the
message of new life in Christ and the life-changing power
of the Holy Spirit.

Wesley's itinerant preaching ministry made him the most
widely traveled man in England. Through him and his
helpers, God worked divine deliverance in the lives of many
people, especially those beyond the pale of the established
Church. Informed historians maintain that the Wesleyan
spiritual renewal saved England from the kind of anti-
religious impulses that brought chaos and the French Revolution in 1789. Wesley's message was profound in its
implications, simple in its presentation, and inclusive in its
scope.

We can encapsulate John Wesley's message under five
themes, each using the word *all*. (1) All need to be saved;
(2) all may be saved; (3) all can know they are saved; (4) all
can be saved from the power of sin; and (5) all are saved to
glorify God and serve others. Charles Wesley, in many
hymns, versified the message of God's power to transform
every human life, even the worst reprobates:

Jesus! the name to sinners dear,
the name to sinners given;

it scatters all their guilty fear,
it turns their hell to heaven.

. . . .

O that the world might taste and see
the riches of his grace!
The arms of love that compass me
would all the world embrace.

John Wesley excelled as a preacher, writer, administrator, ecumenist, and theologian. By any standard, his distinction is firmly fixed. Even his severest critics acknowledged his abilities. An opposing bishop said, "He was formed of the best stuff Nature ever put into a fanatic." Wesley appealed to "men of reason and religion" as well as to the uneducated and crude citizens of the nation. He was a keen theologian, and he broadcast his theology not in books of systematic theology but in easily grasped sermons. He took seriously the teachings his Church professed to believe—namely, those found in its Articles of Religion, its Collects, and its Homilies. For him, theology was not an end but a means to communicate the biblical revelation to all people, whatever their social state or moral condition.

John Wesley was an evenhanded religious thinker. He balanced divine sovereignty and human freedom, doctrine and Christian experience, right belief and right conduct, personal religion and its social expression, traditional liturgy and innovative forms. This DVD—*Wesley: A Heart Transformed Can Change the World*—brings Wesley to us with fresh authenticity. Wesley was, and continues to be, both a theological and a spiritual mentor to many.

After many years of unfair criticism, in due time John Wesley gained acknowledgment for his personal attributes and effective ministries. Westminster Abbey memorialized him as a distinguished figure of compelling excellence. Artists have produced more portraits and engravings of him than of any other person in English history, and painters and sculptors continue to create likenesses of him. *The Cambridge Modern History*, in its volume on the eighteenth century, concludes, "In universality of influence and in range of achievement, he was more important than any." *The Oxford Dictionary of the Christian Church* states, "John Wesley was one of the greatest Christians of his age."

Wesley's small book *The Character of a Methodist* stressed what is at the heart of Christianity. He declared:

A Methodist is one who has "the love of God shed abroad in his heart by the Holy Ghost given unto him"; one who "loves the Lord his God with all his heart, and with all his soul, and with all his mind, and with all his strength." God is the joy of his heart, and the desire of his soul; which is constantly crying out, "Whom have I in heaven but thee? and there is none upon earth that I desire beside thee! My God and my all! Thou art the strength of my heart, and my portion for ever!"

Those familiar with the Bible recognize the plethora of biblical citations and allusions in his writings.

Wesley was confident of the veracity of his sermons because he drew them from Scripture. For him, the Bible was not a compilation of human theories; it was a divine revelation inspired by the Holy Spirit. In the often-quoted preface to his sermons he wrote:

> I am a spirit come from God, and returning to God: Just hovering over the great gulf; till, a few moments hence, I am no more seen; I drop into an unchangeable eternity! I want to know one thing—the way to heaven; how to land safe on that happy shore. God himself has condescended to teach the way: For this very end he came from heaven. He hath written it down in a book. O give me that book! At any price, give me the book of God! I have it: Here is knowledge enough for me. Let me be [a man of one book].

At another time, he stated, "I must declare just what I find in the Book."

Wesley often warned against the danger of depending only on the imputed righteousness of Christ, to the neglect of Christ's imparted righteousness that leads to a holy life, inwardly and outwardly. He declared that the sanctification of Christian believers is "the grand depositum" of Methodism for the benefit of the universal Church. He told his converts, "Christ cannot *reign* where sin *reigns*." Victory over sin, Wesley insisted, comes not from human effort, but entirely from God's grace mediated by the Holy Spirit. Holiness is not a human achievement; it's a divine gift.

Wesley's definition of holiness was uncomplicated. "It is," he said, "the life of God in the soul of man" (Galatians 2:20). He defined holiness as "the renewal of our heart after the image of Him that created us" (Colossians 3:10). Wesley said to John Newton (the author of the hymn "Amazing Grace") that holiness is "salvation from all sin and loving God with an undivided heart" (Psalm 86:11). Wesley wrote, "I have learned that true Christianity consists, not in a set of opinions, or of forms and ceremonies, but in holiness of heart and life—in a thorough imitation of our divine Master" (1 Peter 2:21). He defined holiness as "having, not some part only, but all the mind which was in him; and of walking as he walked, not only in many or in most respects, but in all things."

John Wesley insisted that true religion is an individual relationship between God and the trusting worshiper. He believed that the Christian life is not merely a contract between God and a Christian believer. So far as it goes, that statement is true. However, the Christian life is a relationship between the believer and God. This relationship leads to forgiveness for our sins and victory over the power of sin. Wesley's definitions of the Christian life echo that of the angelic messenger's announcement to Joseph in a vision: "Don't be afraid to take Mary as your wife, because the child she carries was conceived by the Holy Spirit. She will give birth to a son, and you will call him Jesus, because he will save his people from their sins" (Matthew 1:20-21 CEB).

In a letter to John Wesley, the Bishop of London asked him what is meant by the biblical phrase "a perfect man." Wesley replied:

We understand . . . "a perfect man" [to be] one in whom God hath fulfilled his faithful word: "From all your filthiness, and from all your idols, will I cleanse you. I will also save you from all your uncleanness." We understand hereby, one whom God hath sanctified throughout, even in "body, soul, and spirit"; one who "walketh in the light, as He is in the light," in whom "is no darkness at all"; the blood of Jesus Christ his Son having "cleansed him from all sin."

This statement was and is John Wesley's message to the world.

SESSION 1
John Wesley: Seeker after God

■■■ INTRODUCTION

Half jestingly and half seriously, it has been said that the family from which John and Charles Wesley sprang was partially healthy, never wealthy, and sometimes wise. Regarding *health*, only ten of the nineteen children born to Susanna and Samuel Wesley survived infancy. As for *wealth*, the family lived in virtual poverty, and often Susanna Wesley did not know where the next family meal would come from. In the matter of *wisdom*, the parents sometimes made mistakes with their children (treating them as small adults). Despite a less than ideal home, Samuel and Susanna Wesley bequeathed to their children a well-above-average intellectual and spiritual heritage. Two of the Wesley children became persons of renown. John Wesley was the most important religious leader in eighteenth-century England, and Charles Wesley's poetic gifts enabled him to write some of Christianity's most enduring hymns.

Samuel Wesley, the father, was an Oxford-educated scholar, a Church of England rector, and a poet. One of the few of Samuel's papers that survived the 1709 fire that destroyed the Epworth rectory was his hymn "Behold the Savior of Mankind," which appears in the 1989 *United Methodist Hymnal*. Samuel tutored his sons in Latin and Greek, also teaching them the art of verse. His chief concern was to teach his children about God. When the sixty-nine-year-old Samuel Wesley lay dying, he said to John, "The inward witness, son, the inward witness—this is the proof, the strongest proof, of Christianity." The old man laid his hand on the head of Charles and exclaimed, "Be steady! The Christian faith will surely revive in this kingdom; you shall see it, though I shall not."

Susanna Wesley had a profound influence on her children. A British scholar described her as "very beautiful, and very clever, and very good." John Wesley was her fifteenth child, and Charles Wesley was her eighteenth. She remained serene even through multiple pregnancies and the household's continual poverty. As soon as her children could speak, she taught them the Lord's Prayer. Early in childhood, they memorized portions of the Church of England's *Book of Common Prayer*. Susanna devoted six hours a day to home-schooling her children (she wrote her own curriculum). She diligently attended to their religious nurture (weekly, she met privately with each of her offspring). She kept a journal, wrote letters, educational and catechetical writings, and commentaries on the Apostles' Creed and the Ten Commandments. Even in John Wesley's adult life, he continued to consult with his mother for counsel and advice.

In 1724 she wrote John, then at Oxford, about his struggle to find the full assurance of faith. Her letter said, "Happy are you . . . now in good earnest resolve to make religion the business of your life. For, after all, that is the one thing that strictly speaking is necessary. . . . I heartily wish you would now enter upon a serious examination of yourself, that you may know whether you have a reasonable hope of salvation by Jesus Christ, that is, whether you are in a state of faith and repentance or not." Less than two years before Susanna died, she wrote Charles Wesley: "I know not what other opinion people may have of human nature, but for my part I think that without the grace of God we are utterly incapable of thinking, speaking or doing anything good." Susanna Wesley was one of the greatest mothers in the history of the English people.

At the age of ten and a half years, John Wesley was sent by his parents to Charterhouse, a respected boarding school in London. There, he received an excellent education in classical literature, especially in Latin and Greek. His six years at Charterhouse prepared him to enter Oxford's Christ Church College in January of 1720. Because of John's scholarly achievements, in 1726 the university's Lincoln College elected him a fellow. He taught Greek, moral philosophy, and Scripture. He also diligently included religious instruction in his tutoring, hoping to make his students better men. He allowed himself some social diversions, yet he put religion first. He arose between 4:00 and 5:00 a.m. daily to read the Scriptures and pray. His work at Oxford's Lincoln College earned him respect as a superior tutor.

While at Lincoln College, Wesley read the works of several German Pietists who stressed the lordship of Christ and the guidance of the Holy Spirit. They also emphasized the importance of overcoming the fear of death and the opinions of others. He had not yet experienced a personal spiritual transformation, called "the new birth." He said, "I saw the indispensable necessity of having the mind which was in Christ and of walking as He walked . . . in all things."

Wesley's reading of Christian devotional writers encouraged him to seek entire sanctification. He wrote, "I [took communion] every week. I watched against all sin, whether in word or deed. I began to aim at, and pray for inward holiness." Yet Wesley felt depressed because he fell short of the spiritual goals he sought. Time and again, he wrote in his diary about his weaknesses, such as idleness and undisciplined reading. He set rules and regulations for himself, with the hope they would better his life and make him more pleasing to God. His concerns with trifles reveal that he was too introspective and that he trusted in his own efforts more than in Jesus Christ.

At Oxford he joined the "Holy Club" and soon became its leader. The group read the Latin and Greek classics, lived austerely, and gave sacrificially to the poor. They also visited jails and, out of their own meager incomes, provided prisoners with religious literature, food, clothing, and coal. Many were in prison due to their debts, and the Holy Club raised money to pay their creditors. The prisoners' families often lived with them in the jails, and the members of the Holy Club started a school for the inmates' children. The members of the club observed all the church year's designated fasts, which few of the other university students or professors kept. Wesley and his friends attended almost every service of Holy Communion, in the hope that their religious observances and good works would bring them the assurance of salvation.

Opposition came to the members of the Holy Club, chiefly because the lives of its members were unspoken rebukes to the casual faith and undisciplined lives of the majority of the university community. Wesley's diaries substantiate his spiritual uneasiness. He often asked himself, "How can I love God with my whole heart? How can I achieve holiness of heart and life?" He read two books by William Law, whose writings recommended self-denial and acts of mortification. Law talked about a life of renunciation—including the rejection of popular literature, masquerades, playing cards, and the theatre.

Although Wesley enjoyed the academic atmosphere of Oxford, he suffered inner turmoil because of his unhappy spiritual state. His prayers seemed to bounce off an impenetrable ceiling. He lacked a sense of God's pardon, favor, and blessing, and he had no assurance that he was a true Christian.

Wesley's career took a new direction when he met General James Oglethorpe, who offered him a position as chaplain of a newly chartered British colony in Georgia. Wesley's chief reason for accepting the post was to save his own soul. He wrote, "I hope to learn the true sense of the gospel of Christ by preaching it to the 'heathen.' " Charles Wesley grudgingly agreed to sail with John to Georgia, where

Charles would serve as secretary to General Oglethorpe. Like John, Charles lacked the personal assurance of Christ's grace and favor. From Georgia, he wrote a friend, "In vain have I fled from myself to Georgia. . . . Go where I will, I carry my Hell about me."

Twenty-six Moravians from Germany, led by Bishop David Nitschmann, sailed on the same ship as the Wesleys. During the stormy voyage to Georgia, John Wesley learned how much he feared death. He wrote in his journal: "I could not but say to myself, 'How is it that thou hast no faith?' being still unwilling to die." The Moravian Christians, by contrast, calmly sang hymns during the storm at sea. John Wesley was deeply impressed by the serene faith of the German Christians, which contrasted with the fear that gripped the English passengers.

Wesley sought spiritual counsel from one of their leaders, August Spangenberg. This Moravian minister probed Wesley with questions. "Have you the witness within yourself?" he asked. Wesley did not understand what Spangenberg meant, and he asked for clarification. The German responded with another question: "Does the Spirit of God bear witness with your spirit that you are a child of God?" Wesley hesitated to reply. Spangenberg persisted, "Do you know Jesus Christ?" Wesley said, "I know he is the Savior of the world."

"True," Spangenberg rejoined. "But do you know he has saved you?" Wesley falteringly replied, "I hope he has died to save me." Gently, Spangenberg asked, "Do you know yourself?" Wesley said uncomfortably, "I do." Later, however, Wesley scribbled in his journal, "I fear they were vain words." Without saying so, both Spangenberg and Wesley knew that Wesley could not honestly testify that Jesus Christ was his personal savior. Not until after John and Charles Wesley returned to England did they experience the certainty and joy of the inner witness of the Holy Spirit to their salvation.

Thus, John Wesley learned from his spiritual disquiet and from his disappointing ministry in Georgia that good intentions, self-effort, and sacrificial good works cannot make one a Christian. His life experiences confirmed to him that the best of good intentions and human efforts cannot overcome the sinful nature with which we are born. Wesley had not given due attention to the doctrine of original sin.

The ninth article of Anglicanism's Thirty-nine Articles of Religion states that original sin "is the fault and corruption of the Nature of every man, that naturally is engendered of the offspring of Adam; whereby man is very far gone from original righteousness, and is of his own nature inclined to evil, so that the flesh lusteth always contrary to the Spirit." American Methodism's Confession of Faith states: "[We] believe [we are] fallen from righteousness and, apart from the grace of our Lord Jesus Christ, [are] destitute of holiness and inclined to evil. . . . Without divine grace, [we] cannot do good works pleasing and acceptable to God." Wesley still did not adequately comprehend that we cannot work our way into God's favor. Salvation is God's gift to be received by faith.

PRAYER CONCERNS

After praying for expressed concerns, the group may pray together the following prayer:

Eternal God, you have placed eternity in our hearts, and we can find our rest and our salvation in you alone. We have strayed like lost sheep, and we all have gone our own way. Yet, without you, there is no lasting happiness or joy. We thank you that you seek us long before we seek you. You draw us to yourself by your Holy Spirit, and in your mercy and grace you promise to forgive us and adopt us as your sons and daughters. We open ourselves to your saving love, and we thank you that you have promised to save all who turn to you in repentance and faith. We pray through Christ your eternal son and our everlasting Lord. Amen.

 **SCRIPTURE**

I will bless the LORD at all times;
  his praise shall continually be in my mouth.
My soul makes its boast in the LORD;
  let the humble hear and be glad.
O magnify the LORD with me,
  and let us exalt his name together.

I sought the LORD, and he answered me,
  and delivered me from all my fears.
Look to him, and be radiant;
  so your faces shall never be ashamed.

This poor soul cried, and was heard by the LORD,
and was saved from every trouble.
The angel of the LORD encamps
around those who fear him, and delivers them.
(Psalm 34:1-7 NRSV)

"Come to me, all you who are struggling hard and carrying heavy loads, and I will give you rest. Put on my yoke, and learn from me. I'm gentle and humble. And you will find rest for yourselves. My yoke is easy to bear, and my burden is light." (Matthew 11:28-30 CEB)

 DVD

View the DVD from the start until John Wesley leaves Georgia to return to England. Note the ways that he relied on his own effort and good works to earn the assurance of God's favor.

GROUP DISCUSSION AND POINTS TO PONDER

1. Why did the highly religious and morally upright John Wesley lack the assurance of God's favor? (Ephesians 2:8-9; John 6:28-29)
2. Discuss the differences between the "hot-blooded sins of the flesh" and the "cold-blooded sins of the spirit."
3. What were the chief causes of John Wesley's religious uncertainty and his lack of a sense of God's presence in his life? (Philippians 3:9; Hebrews 11:6)

4. In what ways did John Wesley's mother influence his search for God? Talk about our spiritual responsibility for our children. (Deuteronomy 4:9; 2 Timothy 1:5)

5. Did John Wesley's leadership gifts help or hinder his search for the assurance of God's favor and blessing?

6. Evaluate John Wesley's statements as a frustrated seeker: "By suffering we come to know God" and "My salvation lies in taking the gospel to others." (Matthew 7:22-23; Titus 3:5-7)

7. Discuss in what ways John Wesley's narrow escape from the fire at the Epworth rectory influenced the direction of his life. Has some near catastrophe affected your life in a significant way?

8. In what ways do you think the poverty of the Epworth household influenced John Wesley's ministry?

9. How important is the inner witness of the Holy Spirit that we are in right relationship with God? (Romans 8:16; Galatians 4:6; 1 John 3:24)

10. Discuss our human tendency to try to earn God's favor. (Romans 3:20; 10:1-3; Galatians 5:4-5)

SUGGESTED CHARLES WESLEY HYMN (*THE UNITED METHODIST HYMNAL*, 1989)
Hymn #88, "Maker, in Whom We Live"

CLOSING PRAYER

God, our Father, we thank you for your faithfulness through the ages. Before the mountains were formed or you brought forth the universe and the earth, from everlasting to everlasting you are God. Your will, your word, and your way remain ever constant. Your compassions never fail; they are new every morning; great is your faithfulness. We thank you for the life of your servant John Wesley. May we also become obedient to your call, dedicated to your will, and fully involved in your plan to create a new and transformed humanity. To that end we entrust ourselves into your care and keeping, through Jesus Christ the Lord of life. Amen.

SESSION 2
Inner Transformation by God's Grace

■■■ INTRODUCTION

In all, John Wesley's ministry in America proved disappointing. His rigid ways and formal churchmanship were not suited to the colonists. He insisted on triune immersion for baptism; he refused to conduct the burial service for a non-Anglican. His bungled love affair with Sophia Hopkey and his ill-considered act of denying her the sacrament of Communion resulted in a civil indictment against him.

Furthermore, Wesley had not been able to preach to the Choctaw Indians as he had hoped. The few times he spoke to them failed to arouse any positive response. Defeated and disillusioned, he fled Savannah and sailed back to England. On the ship *Samuel*, the depressed John Wesley pondered his spiritual state and future ministry. He was too disheartened to preach to the ship's passengers and crew, as he had done earlier during his voyage to Georgia.

As the *Samuel* approached England, Wesley wrote in his journal: "I went to America, to convert the Indians; but Oh! who shall convert me? Who . . . will deliver me from this evil heart of unbelief? I have a fair summer religion. . . . But let death look me in the face, and my spirit is troubled" (*Works of John Wesley*, vol. 18, p. 211). He reflected, "In a storm I think, 'What if the Gospel be not true?' Then thou art of all men most foolish. . . . For what art thou wandering over the face of the earth? A dream, 'a cunningly-devised fable'? O who will deliver me from this fear of death! What shall I do? Where shall I fly from it?" (ibid.)

Wesley's self-sacrificing labors had gained him no peace or freedom from the fear of death. He wrote, "It is now two years and almost four months since I left my native country. . . . But what have I learned myself in the meantime? Why (what I the least of all suspected), that I who went to America to convert others, was never myself converted to God" (ibid., p. 214). Wesley returned to Oxford, still as a fellow of Lincoln College. His main preoccupation was to win God's acceptance and favor. His former self-confidence had dwindled, and he felt far from God.

At this point, Wesley met a new friend named Peter Böhler, a German Pietist. To bridge the language gap between them, they communicated in Latin about spiritual matters. Böhler carefully explained to John and Charles Wesley the distinction between two contrasting ways: (1) relying on self-effort to earn God's approval through good deeds and sacrificial service, which contrasted with (2) receiving salvation by faith alone that trusts in God's unmerited love and saving grace. The first way trusts in what we do; the second way trusts in what Christ did on the cross. One way says, *Do*; the other way says, *Done*.

Both Wesley brothers puzzled over whether we can be justified by Christ in a moment, only by trusting in God's grace alone, as an undeserving penitent. At the outset, John Wesley's logical and classically trained mind balked at the idea of instantaneous conversion by faith alone. He did not comprehend how one could become a Christian so simply. Christian theology identifies the source of our stubborn tendency to resist submission of ourselves as stemming from "original sin" or our "fallen nature."

Wesley asked Peter Böhler for proof of instantaneous conversions by faith alone. Böhler retorted that such conversions were common in the book of Acts and in the early church. "What reasons have I to believe [God] works in the same manner now?" Wesley probed (ibid., p. 234).

Böhler invited Wesley to hear the testimonies of a number of people who bore witness to their instantaneous conversions. Although Wesley was not convinced that salvation was so uncomplicated, he was willing to listen to such witnesses. Each of them testified from personal experience that faith in Christ brought them certain assurance of God's pardon. Böhler wrote that Wesley was "struck dumb" by these testimonies.

Still, Wesley was not fully convinced that God will pardon us in a moment. Meanwhile, Böhler decided to leave England to become a missionary in South Carolina. Before sailing, he sent Wesley an impassioned letter:

> I love you greatly, and think much of you in my journey, wishing and praying that the tender mercies of Jesus Christ . . . may be manifested to your soul: that you may taste, and then see, how exceedingly the Son of God has loved you. . . . Beware of the sin of unbelief; and if you have not conquered it yet, see that you conquer it this very day, through the blood

of Jesus Christ. Delay not, I beseech you, to believe in *your* Jesus Christ; but so put him in mind of his promises to poor sinners that he may not be able to refrain from doing for you what he hath done for so many others. . . . Surely he is now ready to help; and nothing can offend him but our unbelief. Believe therefore. (*Works of John Wesley*, vol. 18, p. 239)

Wesley admitted to himself that the New Testament contains accounts of instant conversion. He also contemplated the compelling evidence which he saw in the lives of many Christians who witnessed "with one mouth that this faith was the . . . free gift of God" (ibid., p. 248). Gradually, Wesley became persuaded that the fundamental truth of Christianity is that for salvation we must trust God for everything and ourselves for nothing. He wrote in his journal, "I was now thoroughly convinced. And, by the grace of God, I resolved to seek it unto the end." Some of Wesley's friends and his brother Samuel worried over his new religious fervor. Nonetheless, both John and Charles Wesley began to pray in earnest for salvation by grace through faith.

Four influences moved the two brothers toward their evangelical conversions:

(1) *Reading.* Their study of *A Serious Call to a Devout and Holy Life* by William Law, and *The Life of God in the Soul of Man* by Henry Scougal, deeply impressed them of the possibility of an inward transformation that comes from trusting Jesus Christ as Savior.

(2) *Preaching.* The sermons of George Whitefield, who had been a member of the Oxford Holy Club, deeply moved the two brothers. Whitefield had trusted Christ for salvation in the spring of 1735, and he had become an earnest Christian and an exceptionally effective evangelist. His famous sermon "Ye Must Be Born Again" was read widely and often preached with astonishing success.

(3) *Conversations.* A third influence on John and Charles Wesley was the series of discussions they had with such Moravian Pietists as Count Nicholas von Zinzendorf and Peter Böhler.

(4) *Witnesses.* The personal testimonies of scores of Christians to a new birth by faith in Jesus Christ were gripping. For instance, Charles Wesley wrote about John Bray, "a poor ignorant mechanic, who knows nothing but Christ, yet by knowing him, knows and discerns all things. . . . We prayed together for faith. I was quite overpowered and melted into tears."

John and Charles, each in his own way, came to see that justification by faith was not a new doctrine but rather a fundamental teaching of Scripture, the ancient church, and the Protestant Reformation. On May 21, 1738, Charles was the first of the two brothers to experience salvation by faith alone. On the evening of his evangelical conversion, he wrote, "I was in a new heaven and a new earth!" He wrote a hymn to celebrate his new life in Christ. One stanza reads:

And can it be that I should gain
an interest in the Savior's blood!
Died he for me? who caused his pain!
For me? who him to death pursued?
Amazing love! How can it be
that thou, my God, shouldst die for me?

Thereafter, Charles Wesley wrote thousands of hymns, which are rooted in scriptural Christianity, brimming with joyful praise to Jesus Christ, keenly personal (frequently using personal pronouns), and expressive of the joyful assurance and hope of those who have trusted in Christ as the sole means of salvation.

John Wesley heard the news of Charles's spiritual victory, and wrote in his journal: "I received the surprising news that my brother had found rest to his soul." However, John spiritually agonized for three more days. With heavy heart, he realized he was a needy sinner, and he saw that all his spiritual austerity and good works were without merit. He came to see that he had nothing to offer God other than his willingness to surrender to the lordship of Christ.

John continued to seek after Christ, and on May 24, 1738 at 5:00 a.m. he awakened and read from his Greek New Testament: "There are given unto us exceeding great and precious promises, even that ye should be partakers of the divine nature, having escaped the corruption that is in the world through lust" (2 Peter 1:4, *Works of John Wesley*, vol. 18). In the late afternoon, he attended St. Paul's Cathedral and was encouraged by the words of an anthem: "Out of the deep have I called unto thee, O Lord."

In the evening he went "very unwillingly" to a meeting of a Moravian society on London's Aldersgate Street. A leader read from Martin Luther's Preface to the Epistle to the Romans a passage describing "the change which God works in the heart through faith in Christ." During the reading, God transformed John Wesley's life. Recalling the experience, he later wrote, "I felt I did trust in Christ, Christ alone for salvation, and an assurance was given me that he had taken away *my* sins, even *mine*, and saved *me* from the law of sin and death" (*Works of John Wesley*, vol. 18, p. 250). On the evening of John Wesley's heart-warming experience, he and a group of friends rushed to tell Charles Wesley about John's life-changing transformation.

Charles's journal tells what happened: "Towards ten [p.m.], my brother was brought in triumph by a troop of our friends, and declared, 'I believe.' We sang the hymn with great joy, and parted with prayer." Probably, the hymn they sang was an eight-stanza hymn Charles had newly composed. Two of the verses read:

Where shall my wondering soul begin?
How shall I all to heaven aspire?
A slave redeemed from death and sin,
a brand plucked from eternal fire,
how shall I equal triumphs raise,
and sing my great deliverer's praise?

O how shall I the goodness tell,
Father, which Thou to me hast showed?
That I, a child of wrath and hell,
I should be called a child of God!
Should know, should feel my sins forgiven,
blest with this antepast of heaven!

The following day, John Wesley entered into his journal: "This I know, I have *now peace with God.*"

In 1738 the two brothers began preaching ministries, which led to the famed Wesleyan revival that birthed Methodism, brought tens of thousands to faith in Christ, and eventually led to an evangelical wing within the Anglican Church.

 PRAYER CONCERNS

After praying for expressed concerns, the group may pray together the following prayer:

Lord, Creator of all things, we acknowledge that you are all powerful, all loving, and sovereign over the lives of us all. We recognize our dependence on you, for in you we live and move and have our being. Without your grace and care we would utterly perish. Forgive our foolish dependence on ourselves to live rightly so as to merit a place in the world to come. We confess our dependence on your undeserved favor and transforming power for all you intend for us to be and to do. Help us honor you in everything large and small. We pray through Jesus Christ, the Lord of life and the only Savior of the world. Amen.

SCRIPTURE READING

All who are led by God's Spirit are God's sons and daughters. You didn't receive a spirit of slavery to lead you back again into fear, but you received a Spirit that shows you are adopted as his children. With this Spirit, we cry, "Abba, Father." The same Spirit agrees with our spirit, that we are God's children. But if we are children, we are also heirs. We are God's heirs and fellow heirs with Christ, if we really suffer with him so that we can also be glorified with him. (Romans 8:14-17 CEB)

But when the fulfillment of the time came, God sent his Son, born through a woman, and born under the Law. This was so he could redeem those under the Law so that we could be adopted. Because you are sons and daughters, God sent the Spirit of his Son into our hearts, crying, "Abba, Father." Therefore you are no longer a slave but a son or daughter, and if you are his child, then you are also an heir through God. (Galatians 4:4-7 CEB)

SCENES FROM THE DVD

View scenes from the DVD from the point of Wesley's return to England and his heart-warming experience of the assurance of his salvation.

 GROUP DISCUSSION AND POINTS TO PONDER

1. Discuss one or more of the following instances of saving faith in the New Testament:
   - Zacchaeus (Luke 19:1-10)
   - A man from Ethiopia (Acts 8:26-38)

- Saul of Tarsus (Acts 22:3-16)
- Lydia (Acts 16:11-15)
- A jailer at Philippi (Acts 16:29-34)

2. Did Jesus Christ die that all people can be saved, or did he die only for certain elect individuals? (Luke 11:10; John 3:16-18; Acts 10:34-35; Romans 2:10–11:12; Revelation 22:17)

3. Why do some people hunger for and respond to God, while others do not? (John 3:17-20)

4. Discuss spiritual pride, self-will, and their end result. (Luke 18:11; John 9:41; Romans 10:1-4; Revelation 3:17)

5. Can we reconcile the biblical commands to "fear God" and "be not afraid"?

    ("*Fear of God*": Deuteronomy 10:12; Joshua 24:14; Isaiah 8:13; 1 Peter 1:17)

    ("*Do Not Fear*": Genesis 16:24; Isaiah 41:10, 43:1; Matthew 10:30-31; Revelation 1:17)

6. Discuss the importance of encouraging those who doubt God, those who have weak faith, and those who have abandoned their faith. (Acts 11:23, 15:32; Hebrews 3:13, 10:24)

7. What effects take place in those who trust in Christ alone for their salvation? (Romans 7:6, 8:11; 2 Corinthians 5:17; Ephesians 2:6, 4:24; Colossians 3:10)

8. Are there many ways of salvation or "roads to heaven"? (John 14:6; Acts 4:12; Romans 5:1-2; Ephesians 3:12-18; Hebrews 10:19-22)

9. In the light of the New Testament, discuss John Wesley's passion for a personal assurance of his salvation (Colossians 2:2-3; 2 Timothy 1:12; Hebrews 10:22; 1 John 4:13)

10. What mistakes and errors did John and Charles Wesley make in their long and torturous search for God's forgiveness and favor?

 **SUGGESTED CHARLES WESLEY HYMN**

Hymn #163, "Ask Ye What Great Thing I Know"

 CLOSING PRAYER

Our Father in heaven, we thank you that your grace extends to all people, times, and circumstances. Forgive us when we question your unfailing love and concern for us. Enter into our lives in your fullness, grace, and love so that we may experience the transforming power of the Lord of life and love—even Jesus Christ, who died for our sins that we might be saved. We unreservedly open ourselves to you, in the name of the risen Lord, who shed his blood for our redemption. Amen.

SESSION 3
The Challenges Wesley Faced

■■■ INTRODUCTION

When John Wesley was thirty-nine, his religious experience at the Aldersgate Street meeting marked the advent of a new and significant fifty-three-year ministry. He would travel some 250,000 miles by horseback and carriage, cross the Irish Channel more than fifty times, and preach more than 40,000 sermons. His now classic journal is widely read today. He also published letters, treatises, expositions of Scripture, translations, tracts, histories, grammars of other languages, and abridgments of classic Christian books. People today still read his works.

John and Charles Wesley, George Whitefield, and their unnumbered followers did not content themselves with bemoaning the cloud of spiritual darkness across England. Rather, they bore witness in word and deed to the good news of God's grace and power. They faithfully proclaimed the good news that Christ came to free us from the bondage of sin and make us holy in character and conduct. Wesley's message included the centrality of repentance, conversion, the witness of the Holy Spirit, and holiness of heart and life. Thousands were transformed by God's grace. By 1740, almost all of England knew about the Reverend John Wesley and the fast-growing Methodist movement.

However, the challenges before Wesley and his followers were vexing—especially so because of the opposition that came from bishops and clergymen of the established Church. Scores of bishops, cathedral deans, and rectors were content to maintain the administrative workings of the institutional church. However, they disliked the religious excitement attending the Wesleyan revival that was spreading across the land. They neglected the essential New Testament message of God's invitation to new life in Christ through repentance and faith. Many clergymen seemed embarrassed to talk about personal religious experience. For these critics, religion ought properly to remain a private matter. Lord Henry Bolingbroke was asked, "What is your religion, my lord?" Bolingbroke replied, "The religion of all sensible men." When asked, "Yes, but what is that?" Bolingbroke declared, "Ah. That is what no sensible man ever tells."

Arthur Hugh Clough, a nineteenth-century poet, summed up the mood of many eighteenth-century people:

> The world is very ill, we see,
> We do not comprehend it.
> But in one point we all agree:
> God won't—and we can't—mend it.

Bishop Joseph Butler believed that "if in [Scripture] there be found any passage, the seeming meaning of which is contrary to natural religion, we may most certainly conclude such seeming meaning not to be the real one."

When John Wesley began his ministry of itinerant preaching soon after his May 24, 1738 heartwarming religious experience, Bishop Butler wrote him a letter of complaint in which he said, "Sir, the pretending to extraordinary revelations and gifts of the Holy Ghost is a horrid thing, a very horrid thing." Wesley replied, "I pretend to no extraordinary revelations or gifts of the Holy Ghost; none but what every Christian may receive, and ought to expect and pray for."

Butler replied, "You have no business here. . . . Therefore, I advise you to go hence." Wesley answered, "My lord, my business on earth is to do what good I can. . . . At present I think I can do most good here; therefore, here I stay." Wesley spent part of his time in Bristol, and he won thousands to Christ there. Butler, the Bishop of Bristol, lived a private life, mostly writing about his philosophical musings. Butler's written works fail to speak of original sin and the need for God's grace to overcome the evil in ourselves and our world. If Butler championed "natural religion," Wesley advocated "revealed religion."

Other bishops and priests pestered Wesley with criticisms and complaints. Wesley stated that the usual cause of such persecution is the cosmic conflict between truth and error. He quoted the words of Jesus: "If you belonged to the world, it would love you as its own. As it is, you do not belong to the world, but I have chosen you out of the world. That is why the world hates you" (John 15:19).

We remember that hostile forces worked against the Old Testament prophets, Jesus, the apostles, and the martyrs. Opposition to scriptural Christianity emerged in Martin

Luther's day and in Wesley's day; and religious persecution continues in our time. Jesus said plainly:

> "This is the basis for judgment: The light came into the world, and people loved darkness more than the light, for their actions are evil. All who do wicked things hate the light and don't come to the light for fear that their actions will be exposed to the light. Whoever does the truth comes to the light so that it can be seen that their actions were done in God." (John 3:19-21 CEB)

Jesus gave a prediction and a promise: "Happy are the people whose lives are harassed because they are righteous, because the kingdom of heaven is theirs" (Matthew 5:10 CEB).

John Wesley was well educated, widely read, and gentlemanly. His speech was controlled, courteous, and cultured. He often spoke against fanaticism, and he made no attempt to inflame people or cause them to rebel against Church authorities. The early Methodist converts became honest, law-abiding, industrious, and charitable toward others. At the least, one would expect that the magistrates and sheriffs would protect them. Such was not the case. Encouraged by Church leaders, the civil authorities harassed and persecuted Wesley and his allies. Wesley was spit upon, beaten, and abused. He advised the Methodists not to return violence for violence.

England's religious officials had two chief objections to Wesley's ministry: (1) He preached in parishes served by others, and (2) he taught that people can know with certainty that God has forgiven and saved them.

Wesley's field preaching throughout England, his use of lay preachers (not approved by bishops), and his network of Methodist societies were outside the control of the institutional Church. Because Anglican pulpits were closed to Wesley, he had no other choice than to preach in the open fields and the Methodist chapels. The practice of field preaching and the widespread successes of the Methodist meetings angered many Anglican priests and bishops.

Wesley's emphasis on the inner assurance that comes from the witness of the Holy Spirit seemed to many Church leaders to be presumptuous and prideful. Church leaders without an inner witness of the Holy Spirit felt scandalized. Regarding the witness of the Holy Spirit in the hearts of believers, Wesley said that he advocated nothing that was not taught in Scripture and in the Articles of the Church. He took at face value those teachings of Scripture that many clerics deemed only "metaphorical." He said, "My ground is the Bible. Yea, I am a Bible-bigot. I follow it in all things, both great and small." Biblical religion, Wesley believed, could and should become real in one's life—and it found lodging in the lives of many, to the consternation of ecclesiastical authorities.

Wesley soldiered onward, despite the hostile winds against him. He was a friend of the poor, and his charitable deeds are legendary. It is probable that no one in England or on the European Continent knew as many people by name as did John Wesley. He encouraged his converts to attend Anglican services to receive the sacraments. The Methodists were careful not to hold their meetings at the same hour as scheduled

Anglican services. Methodist gatherings featured biblical exposition and congregational hymn singing, both of which many Anglican priests neglected.

For more than ten years, ecclesiastical opposition continued against John Wesley. Around 350 anti-Methodist publications came into print before 1762, most of which were unfair or false. Numerous tracts were penned by bishops and priests within Wesley's beloved Anglican Church. Mostly, he ignored these broadsides. He gave his time and energy to disseminate the truth of the Bible and to provide for people's spiritual and physical needs. In the few cases when he believed it was necessary to respond to published criticisms, he did so with courtesy, compelling logic, and biblical support.

The beneficial effects of the Methodist movement were plainly apparent. Honesty, sobriety, and upright living among the Methodists were evident to fair-minded people. Wesley wrote a clergyman: "The habitual drunkard that was, is now temperate in all things; the whoremonger now flees fornication; he that stole, steals no more, but works with his hands; he that cursed or swore, perhaps at every sentence, has now learned to serve the Lord with fear, and rejoice unto him with reverence; those formerly enslaved to various habits of sin are now brought to uniform habits of holiness."

Eventually, Wesley gained respect for his successful ministries. Slowly, he earned the esteem of his former critics, and many of the churches at last opened to him. The transformed lives of so many thousands had improved the morals and manners of England. In 1777, Wesley was welcomed to preach in London's Allhallows Church—a symbolic vindication of his ministry. He wrote, "The congregation seemed to be much affected. . . . It seems, after being scandalous for nearly fifty years, I am at length growing into an honourable man." England's national Church gradually came to recognize the magnitude of Wesley's ministry. From the start, his aim had never been to revile the Church of England, but to renew it.

Gaining recognition and honor did not change John Wesley. He was in no way tempted to bask in the plaudits bestowed on him. To the end of his life, he remained an itinerant preacher. Shortly before he died, he said to a friend, "I have been wandering up and down between fifty and sixty years, endeavoring in my poor way, to do a little good to my fellow-creatures; and now it is probable that there are but a few steps between me and death. . . . I have no other plea than this: 'I the chief of sinners am, but Jesus died for me.'"

As death approached, Wesley began singing a hymn—the one with which he had closed his last service in Methodism's City Road Chapel a week earlier. Others joined him as he sang:

I'll praise my Maker while I've breath;
and when my voice is lost in death,
praise shall employ my nobler powers.
My days of praise shall ne'er be past,
while life, and thought, and being last,
or immortality endures.

John Wesley's dying words were, "The best of all is, God is with us."

OPENING PRAYER

After praying for expressed concerns, the group may pray together the following prayer:

Our Father in heaven, your Son Jesus suffered opposition from the very ones he came to redeem through death on a cross. Your faithful prophets and witnesses have been rejected and despised. Many have suffered martyrdom for their faith, and we pray for unknown numbers of your people who even now undergo opposition in countries around the world. Help us be faithful witnesses to your love, truth, and grace, even in the face of opposition. We pray through Christ our Lord. Amen.

SCRIPTURE READING

"God didn't send his Son into the world to judge the world, but that the world might be saved through him. Whoever believes in him isn't judged; whoever doesn't believe in him is already judged, because they don't believe in the name of God's only Son.

"This is the basis for judgment: The light came into the world, and people loved darkness more than the light, for their actions are evil. All who do wicked things hate the light and don't come to the light for fear that their actions will be exposed to the light. Whoever does the truth comes to the light so that it can be seen that their actions were done in God." (John 3:17-21 CEB)

Don't be afraid of what you are going to suffer. Look! The devil is going to throw some of you into prison in order to test you. You will suffer hardship for ten days. Be faithful even to the point of death, and I will give you the crown of life. (Revelation 2:10 CEB)

DVD

View the portion of the DVD that depicts the period when many clergy and some laity opposed John Wesley and his followers. Observe the causes for the resistance to his ministry. Consider how Wesley responded to unfair treatment.

GROUP DISCUSSION AND POINTS TO PONDER

1. Do we sometimes criticize others who use unfamiliar ways to minister? Can you cite an example of Christians opposing other Christians for the style of their ministries? (Judges 8:1; 1 Samuel 18:8; Matthew 20:12)
2. Why did religious leaders oppose John Wesley's demonstrable successes in turning people from sin to righteousness? (Matthew 7:1; Romans 14:4; 1 Corinthians 4:5)
3. Discuss the ways Jesus Christ and his disciples dealt with false accusations. (Matthew 9:32-36; 11:18-19; Acts 2:13-16, 6:13-15 ff., 24:5-16)
4. How important is it for Christians to work together to win the world for Jesus Christ? (Mark 9:38-39)

5. Discuss the distinction between unorthodox methods and unorthodox teaching.

6. Can you cite instances of people who were sincere but misguided? (Matthew 15:8-9; 1 Timothy 1:7)

7. Persecution against biblical Christianity is strong in some countries. Are Christians discriminated against or persecuted in North America?

8. Talk about our tendency to criticize others who have ministries more outwardly successful than ours. (Matthew 7:4; John 1:46)

9. After viewing the DVD, discuss how Wesley dealt with his critics and persecutors.

10. Can you think of mature Christians you know who seem unperturbed and controlled when unjustly treated or criticized?

 SUGGESTED CHARLES WESLEY HYMN

Hymn #561, "Jesus, United by Thy Grace"

 CLOSING PRAYER

Our Father, we thank you that you said to your faithful people, "Never will I leave you; never will I forsake you." Even when we face obstacles and opposition in your service, we know that you are with us. Help us by faith to overcome the world and its evil by steadfast obedience and unwavering confidence in the promise of Christ, who said to his followers: "Surely I am with you always, to the very end of the age." We pray in his name and for his glory. Amen.

SESSION 4
The Legacy Wesley Bequeathed

■■■ **INTRODUCTION**

By the 1760s, almost every English town or village had a Methodist society. Many of these assemblies built chapels, even if British Methodism was not yet a new denomination. The Wesleyan revival reached into numerous lives among the nation's most degraded and lawless people. Entire villages that were formerly shiftless, poor, and dangerous were transformed into law-abiding, temperate, and productive communities. One of England's most respected historians wrote about the lasting legacy of John Wesley: "It is . . . scarcely an exaggeration to say that the scene which took place at the humble meeting in Aldersgate Street forms an epoch in English history. The conviction which then flashed upon one of the most powerful and most active intellects in England is the true source of . . . Methodism."

Several salient features are comprised in Wesley's legacy: ecumenism, religion of the heart, the witness of the Holy Spirit, sanctification, the priesthood of all believers, and practical religion.

Ecumenicism. We have seen that John Wesley held steadfastly to the doctrinal essentials of biblical Christianity, and that he never quibbled over secondary issues. He wrote, "I have no more right to object to a man for holding a different opinion from mine than I have to differ with a man because he wears a wig and I wear my own hair; but if he takes his wig off and shakes the powder in my eyes, I shall consider it my duty to quit of him as soon as possible." Wesley ranks among the most impressive examples of an ecumenical spirit.

Referring to Christians in other denominations, he said, "If God loveth us, we ought also to love one another. . . . Let the points wherein we differ stand aside: there are enough wherein we agree, enough to be the ground of every Christian temper, and of every Christian action." Wesley combined his unwavering commitment to a set of essential theological beliefs with an indisputable liberality toward others who differed with him on minor matters. Wesley commented on Jesus' prayer for his followers, "Holy Father, watch over them in your name, the name you gave me, that they will be one just as we are one" (John 17:11b CEB). He wrote, *"That they may be one*—with us and with each other; one body, separate from the world: *as we are*—by resemblance to us, though not equality."

Religion of the heart. John Wesley said that true religion is "seated in the heart," and that God's law extends "to all our thoughts as well as words and actions." He often warned his hearers and readers that authentic religion does not consist merely of forms, morality, or orthodoxy. Rather, biblical religion is God's grace made personal in individuals, so as to transform their attitudes and actions. Anything else, he insisted, is "wide of the mark."

John Wesley's prose and Charles Wesley's hymns engendered religious affections and irrepressible enthusiasm that flowed from their transformed lives. The Wesleyan revival opened the people to the freedom and ability to love God and others. He said, "Religion is nothing worth, without the religion of the heart; that 'God is a Spirit, and they who worship him must worship him in spirit and in truth;' that, therefore, external worship is lost labour, without a heart devoted to God." Wesley preached, "In a word: Let thy religion be the religion of the heart."

The witness of the Holy Spirit. Wesley said, "I observed many years ago, 'It is hard to find words in the language of men, to explain the deep things of God. Indeed there are none that will adequately express what the Spirit of God works in his children. But perhaps one might say . . . by the testimony of the Spirit, I mean, an inward impression on the soul, whereby the Spirit of God immediately and directly witnesses to my spirit, that I am a child of God; that Jesus Christ hath loved me, and given himself for me; that all my sins are blotted out, and I, even I, am reconciled to God.' "

The inner witness of the Holy Spirit is one of the distinguishing marks of the Wesleyan tradition, although this note is not exclusive to Methodism. Wesley urged that the assurance of faith is the "common privilege" of Christians, although he denied that this inner assurance was essential to our justification by faith. He taught that some have the "faith of a servant," but not yet the "faith of a son." In all instances, he encouraged others to seek the inner witness of the Holy Spirit.

Wesley's support for the testimony of God's Holy Spirit witnessing to the human spirit caused critics to censure him. One detractor pronounced that Wesley and his followers were "rapturous enthusiasts." In response to such criticisms, Wesley denied that one could receive the witness of the Holy Spirit without using the biblically prescribed means of grace or having the fruit of the Spirit in one's life. Wesley rejected the notion that the Church was in possession of the Holy Spirit, which could be received only through the sacraments of institutional Christianity. Wesley's emphasis on the witness of the Spirit is a healthy antidote to both a rationalist religion and sacerdotal religion. Inner assurance, Wesley believed, helps confirm and enliven the personal presence of God in dedicated Christian believers.

Sanctification. John Wesley also championed the oft-neglected doctrine of sanctification, which he described as "holy love" for God and neighbor. Jesus, of course, summarized the two greatest commandments: *"You must love the Lord your God with your whole heart, with your whole being, with your whole strength, and with your whole mind, and love your neighbor as yourself"* (Luke 10:27 CEB). In their sermons and hymns, the Wesleys highlighted these two commandments, explaining that God calls us to have "clean hearts and godly lives."

Comparing justification and sanctification, Wesley said, "By justification we are saved from the guilt of sin, and restored to the favour of God; by sanctification we are saved from the power and root of sin, and restored to the image of God." Wesley further explained sanctification: "It is love excluding sin; love filling the heart, taking up the whole capacity of the soul. It is love 'rejoicing evermore, praying without ceasing, in every thing giving thanks.'"

The Protestant Reformers focused on justification and adoption—favor that God bestows *on* us. Those sixteenth-century Christians proclaimed the important biblical teaching that salvation comes by grace alone and faith alone through Christ alone. John agreed with the Reformers that we reach heaven not by good deeds but by God's grace. Wesley also stressed the importance of sanctification, which is a work of grace that God works *in* us. Wesley was in entire agreement with the sixteenth-century Reformers who saw their mission as leading people to heaven, but in addition, Wesley wanted to bring heaven into people while they were still on the earth.

Wesley wrote that sanctification is "an inward thing, namely, the life of God in the soul of man; a participation of the divine nature; the mind that was in Christ; or, the renewal of our heart, after the image of Him that created us." Sanctification is not a human achievement or a gift of the church. Rather, it is a work of God's grace, received through faith. We can live the holy lives to which God calls us only by the power of the Holy Spirit. St. Paul wrote the

Thessalonian church: "It is God's will that you should be sanctified."

The priesthood of all believers. Another legacy of John Wesley was his emphasis on the dignity of humankind and the unique value of every living soul. He championed lay education, human dignity, and holiness for every individual. The Methodists opened the door to a ministry of the laity that was formerly unknown in England. In the early days of the Methodist spiritual awakening in England, Wesley was at first reluctant to approve lay preachers. Considering the case of Thomas Maxwell, a layman who had begun to preach, he consulted with his mother regarding the wisdom of condoning lay preaching. She said to him, "Take care what you do with this young man, for he is as surely called of God to preach as you are. Examine what have been the fruits of his preaching, and hear him also yourself." Wesley took his mother's advice, and he came to recognize the value of lay preachers and leaders of Methodist class meetings.

One of these laymen was John Nelson, of whom John Wesley wrote:

> From the time of his finding peace with God, it was continually upon his mind that he must return to his native place. . . . His relations and acquaintance soon began to inquire, what he thought of this new faith; and whether he believed there was any such thing as a man's knowing that his sins were forgiven: John told them point-blank, that this new faith, as they called it, was the old faith of the Gospel; and

that he himself was as sure his sins were forgiven, as he could be of the shining of the sun. . . . Some put him upon the proof of the great truths which such inquiries naturally led him to mention; and thus he was brought unawares to quote, explain, compare, and enforce, several parts of Scripture. This he did at first, sitting in his house, till the company increased so that the house could not contain them.

Nelson said, "I still kept hewing stone in the daytime, and preaching every night." With the blessing of John Wesley, many other lay people followed Nelson's example. These zealous lay speakers preached in the fields, homes, barns, and village greens, where they proclaimed the riches of God's grace to thousands of unchurched people. By the time of Wesley's death, in 1791, a sizable company of lay preachers were proclaiming the gospel across the land. A number of Methodist societies throughout England were started by lay people. We saw earlier that it was a layman, John Bray, who led Charles Wesley to put his faith in Christ as Savior. Wesleyan lay preachers brought Methodism to North America.

John Wesley wrote a friend, "What an idle thing is it for you to dispute about lay Preachers! Is not a lay Preacher preferable to a drunken Preacher? to a cursing, swearing Preacher?" Indeed, Methodism's lay workers provided the Wesleyan revival with a base of local stability and widespread support. Lay workers held their neighbors together in Christian bonds of love, caring, and support. The lay-led class meetings lifted the spirits of the depressed, confirmed the faith of the doubting, offered wise counsel to the confused, and restored those who otherwise might have drifted astray from their Christian commitments.

Practical religion. John Wesley also left a legacy of social religion that addressed the material and physical needs of others. He insisted that social improvements are the inevitable result of vital religion, and that our love of others comes from one source only—God's love in our hearts. He said, "As the love of God naturally leads to works of piety [such as prayer and the study of Scripture], so the love of our neighbour naturally . . . inclines us to feed the hungry; to clothe the naked; to visit them that are sick or in prison; to be as eyes to the blind, and feet to the lame; an husband to the widow, a father to the fatherless." Wesley did not divorce spiritual devotion from social applications. Someone summarized Wesley's view of practical religion:

> Do all the good you can,
> By all the means you can,
> In all the ways you can,
> In all the places you can,
> To all the people you can,
> As long as ever you can.

Wesley called on Christians to serve others. In one of his thirteen sermons on Christ's Sermon on the Mount, he said, "Let the light which is in your heart shine in all good works. . . . Cut off all unnecessary expense in food, in furniture, in apparel. Be a good steward of every gift of God, even of these his lowest gifts. Cut off all unnecessary expense of time, all needless or useless employments." Wesley pronounced that it is a sin to indulge one's self, while ignoring those in need of life's basic necessities.

The Methodists established the first Sunday school in England, and Wesley organized free medical dispensaries and an interest-free loan society. It is often said that England escaped a political revolution because it had experienced a spiritual revolution. Wesley also supported initiatives that reformed prisons, suffused clemency and good sense into penal laws, ended the slave trade, and imparted an impulse to educate the masses. He encouraged John Howard in his activities as England's most recognized eighteenth-century exponent of prison reform. "I had the pleasure of a conversation with Mr. Howard," Wesley wrote; "I think one of the greatest men in Europe. Nothing but the mighty power of God can enable him to go through his difficult and dangerous employments." Wesley also encouraged William Wilberforce, a member of parliament, to work to abolish slavery in England. Four days before Wesley died, he wrote Wilberforce, "He who has guided you from your youth up, may continue to strengthen you in this and all things, is the prayer of, Dear Sir, your affectionate servant, John Wesley."

Wesley advised a "comprehensive charity, which contains feeding the hungry, clothing the naked, lodging the stranger; indeed all good works in one; let those animating words be written on your hearts, and sounding in your ears: 'Inasmuch as ye have done it unto one of the least of these, ye have done it unto ME.'" Historically, the eighteenth-century Wesleyan revival ranks high among Christian renewal movements because it was so spiritually vital, powerful, and extensive. This DVD inspires us to consider ways to recover the Wesleyan heritage, engage in spiritually transforming ministries, revive pallid institutional religion, and reverse the march of godlessness that is currently coarsening and degrading Western culture.

 OPENING PRAYER

After praying for expressed concerns, the group may pray together the following prayer:

Our Father in Heaven, we thank you for the now departed prophets, sages, and saints who still speak to us. The influences of their devoted lives inspire us in our generation to be faithful links in the chain of your divine work in the world. Above all, we praise you for your faithfulness, patience, and grace in our lives. Empower us to serve you with heart, head, and hand. Correct and amend our lives according to your will. Meet needs that we do not know we have, and give us grace that we do not fully recognize we need. We pray through Jesus Christ our Lord. Amen.

✝/SCRIPTURE READING

The LORD is merciful and gracious,
   slow to anger and abounding in steadfast love.
He will not always accuse,
   nor will he keep his anger forever.
He does not deal with us according to our sins,
   nor repay us according to our iniquities.
For as the heavens are high above the earth,
   so great is his steadfast love toward those
      who fear him;
as far as the east is from the west,
   so far he removes our transgressions from us.
As a father has compassion for his children,
   so the LORD has compassion for those who fear him.
For he knows how we are made;
   he remembers that we are dust.

As for mortals, their days are like grass;
   they flourish like a flower of the field;
for the wind passes over it, and it is gone,
   and its place knows it no more.
But the steadfast love of the LORD is from everlasting
      to everlasting
   on those who fear him,
   and his righteousness to children's children,
to those who keep his covenant
   and remember to do his commandments.
(Psalm 103:8-18 NRSV)

DVD

View the DVD from the time George Whitefield invited Wesley to come to Bristol to preach in the open fields.

GROUP DISCUSSION AND POINTS TO PONDER

1. As you reflect on the John Wesley DVD, what do think were Wesley's chief concerns, priorities, and goals?

2. Identify and discuss the Wesleyan legacy with regard to theology and practice.

3. Compare Methodism of the eighteenth- and twenty-first centuries. What are the differences? How can we recapture the power and influence of early Methodism?

4. In the light of Christ's teaching about wineskins, what adjustments do we need to make in the church today? (Matthew 9:17)

5. In what ways can we recover the vital spirituality and effectiveness that marked the ministries of John Wesley? (Mark 2:21-22)

6. Is Christian unity important? What is its source? (John 17:18-23; Romans 12:5; Galatians 3:28)

7. In Christian work, why are the church's plans and programs frequently ineffective? What is the authentic foundation for Christian mission and service? (Matthew 18:19)

8. How do today's sermons and hymns compare with those of the early Wesleyan movement?

9. Do you agree or disagree with the statement, *Early Methodism looked upon sin with more horror, sought salvation more earnestly, experienced God's grace more deeply, lived more joyfully, and served others more sacrificially than many Methodists do today?*

10. What do you believe God wants to do in your congregation? What role does God expect each of us to assume in response to the spiritual and moral decline of our nation?

 SUGGESTED CHARLES WESLEY HYMN

Hymn #554, "All Praise to Our Redeeming Lord"

 CLOSING PRAYER

Lord, we thank you for the men and women of God whom you have anointed and used in earlier times to help lead people out of spiritual darkness into your marvelous light. We praise you that Christ promised to build his church, and that the gates of Hades will not overcome it. We renew our dedication to you and pray that we will be faithful to your call on our lives in our generation. We worship you in spirit and in truth, and to that end we open ourselves to be agents of your transforming power so that others can come to know your love. We pray through Jesus Christ, the risen Lord. Amen.